— The Tale Of The —

VAMPIRE RABBIT

Poem and Illustrations by
Michael Quinlyn-Nixon

**Grosvenor House
Publishing Limited**

This book is published by
Grosvenor House Publishing Ltd
Link House
140 The Broadway, Tolworth, Surrey, KT6 7HT.
www.grosvenorhousepublishing.co.uk

This book is a work of fiction. Any resemblance to
people or events, past or present, is purely coincidental.

A CIP record for this book
is available from the British Library

ISBN 978-1-83975-222-3

Dedicated to the great people of
Tyne and Wear (at home and abroad)
and all of my friends who believed I could
write and illustrate my own book, especially
G. C. Adams and Vicky Boddy ~ vampire movie fans!

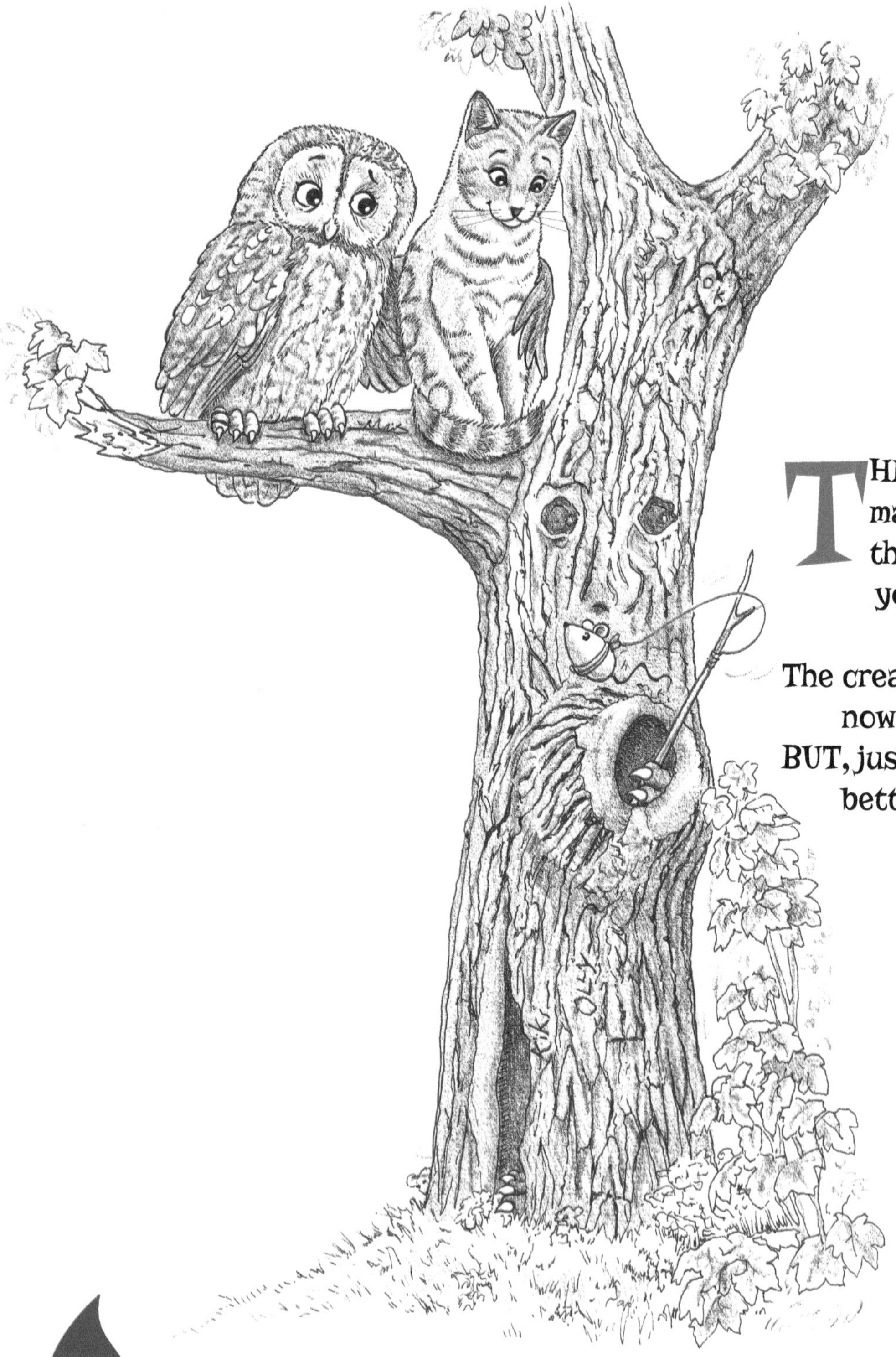
OLLY

THIS tale of blood, claws and fangs
may make you feel queasy,
though the writer hopes
you won't be uneasy.

The creature in this poem is
now 'long-since dead',
BUT, just before you go to sleep,
better CHECK UNDER YOUR BED!

MOUSE

- A NOTE FROM THE AUTHOR AND ILLUSTRATOR -

It is difficult to pinpoint the exact moment when one feels inspired to create something, but it was whilst walking past the 'Vampire Rabbit' almost every Friday morning, for over a year, that I felt the sudden impulse to compose a poem or write a book on the 17th January 2020. A student who is a great fan of all things 'vampire' had, during this time, accompanied me on the trips to Newcastle. I am not so interested in these creatures of the night, it has to be said, having what is deemed a squeamish nature of anything that involves blood or gore!

However, inspiration did come, after gazing up at the Vampire Rabbit grotesque* for the umpteenth time. I was spurred on to almost instantaneous action to write and draw - bitten by the 'creative bug' (not the Vampire Rabbit, thankfully).

When I started this work, I was reminded of my childhood - watching *'The Munsters'* and *'The Addams Family'*, which were great favourites of mine (I didn't see a drop of blood in them), along with the quirky spoof horror movie *'Carry on Screaming',* starring the inimitable talents of **Fenella Fielding**, **Kenneth Williams** and **Harry H. Corbett**.

So, in January, I began the poem which was completed months later on 20th June 2020. Over those five months, I had kept myself very busy, every evening and weekend, drawing images of the Vampire Rabbit (and his unfortunate victims), as well as planning illustrations, doing quite a lot of research and laying out the pages for this book, which is more complicated than you may imagine.

I hope you enjoy the poem and illustrations and please don't lose any sleep about my *'Tale of the Vampire Rabbit'*; I am quite sure these creatures do not really exist (maybe just in the mind of architects, stonemasons and artists!).

M Quinlyn-Nixon

30th June 2020

* A 'grotesque' is the technical term for a style of decorative art containing fanciful, monstrous and quirky human or animal forms, often with foliage. This is in contrast to a gargoyle, which has a waterspout to help preserve stonework from water damage by becoming damp or wet.

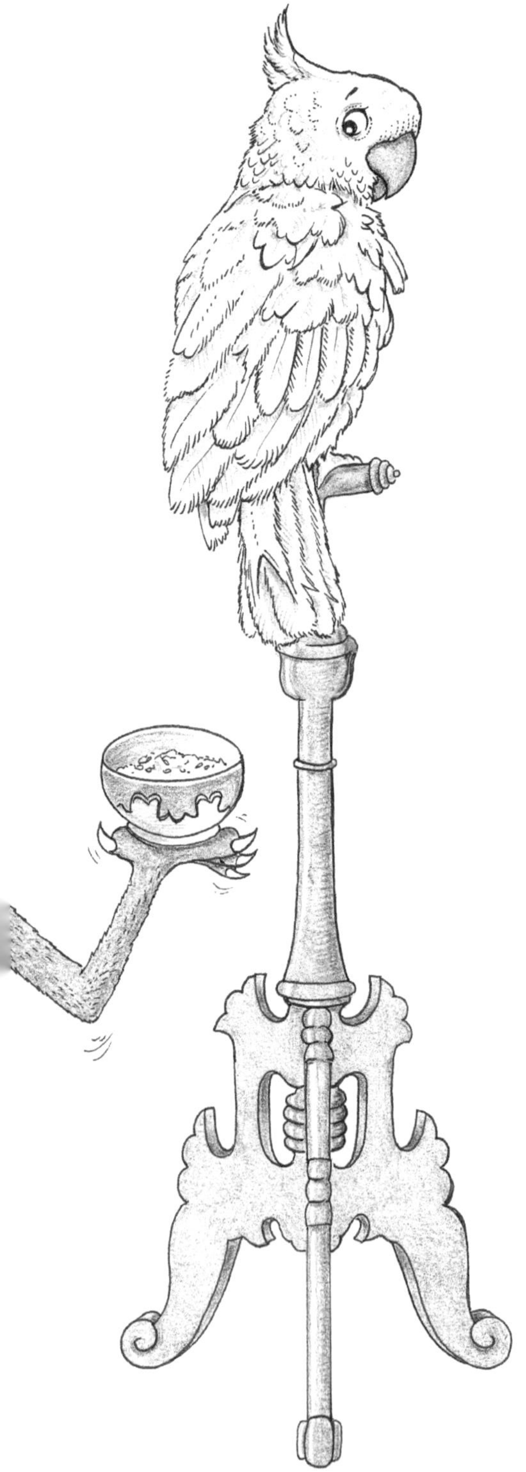

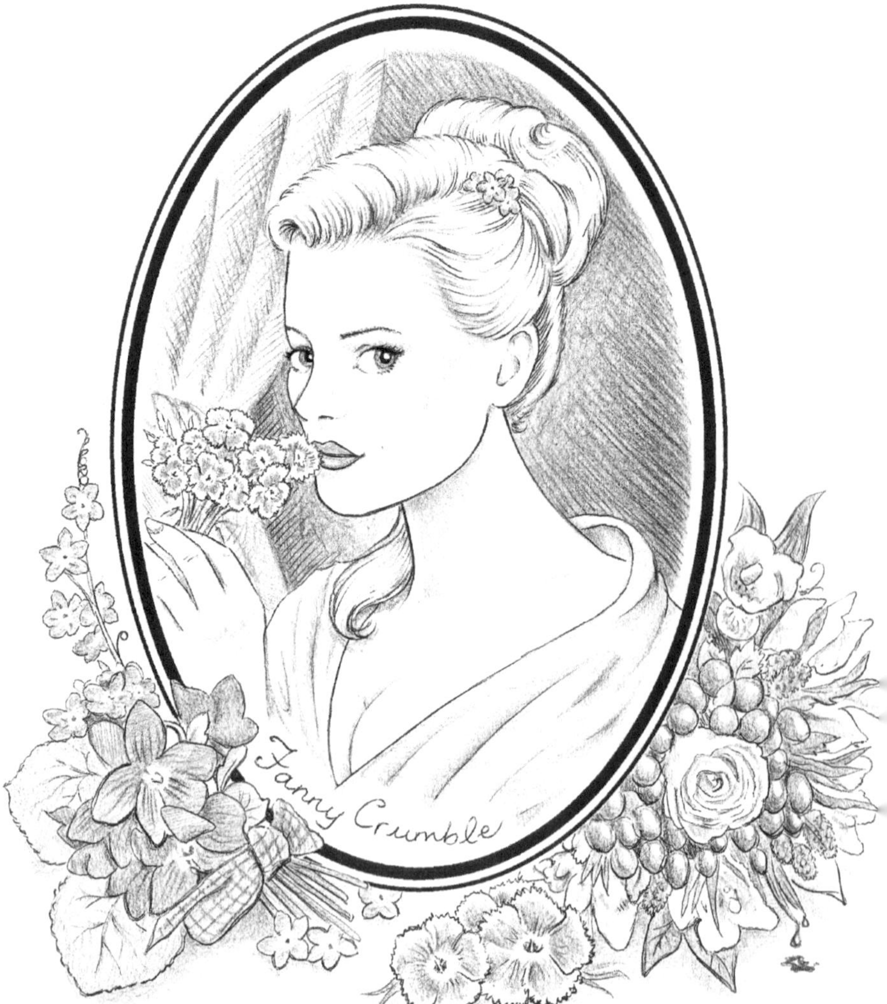
Fanny Crumble

Newcastle upon Tyne

1899

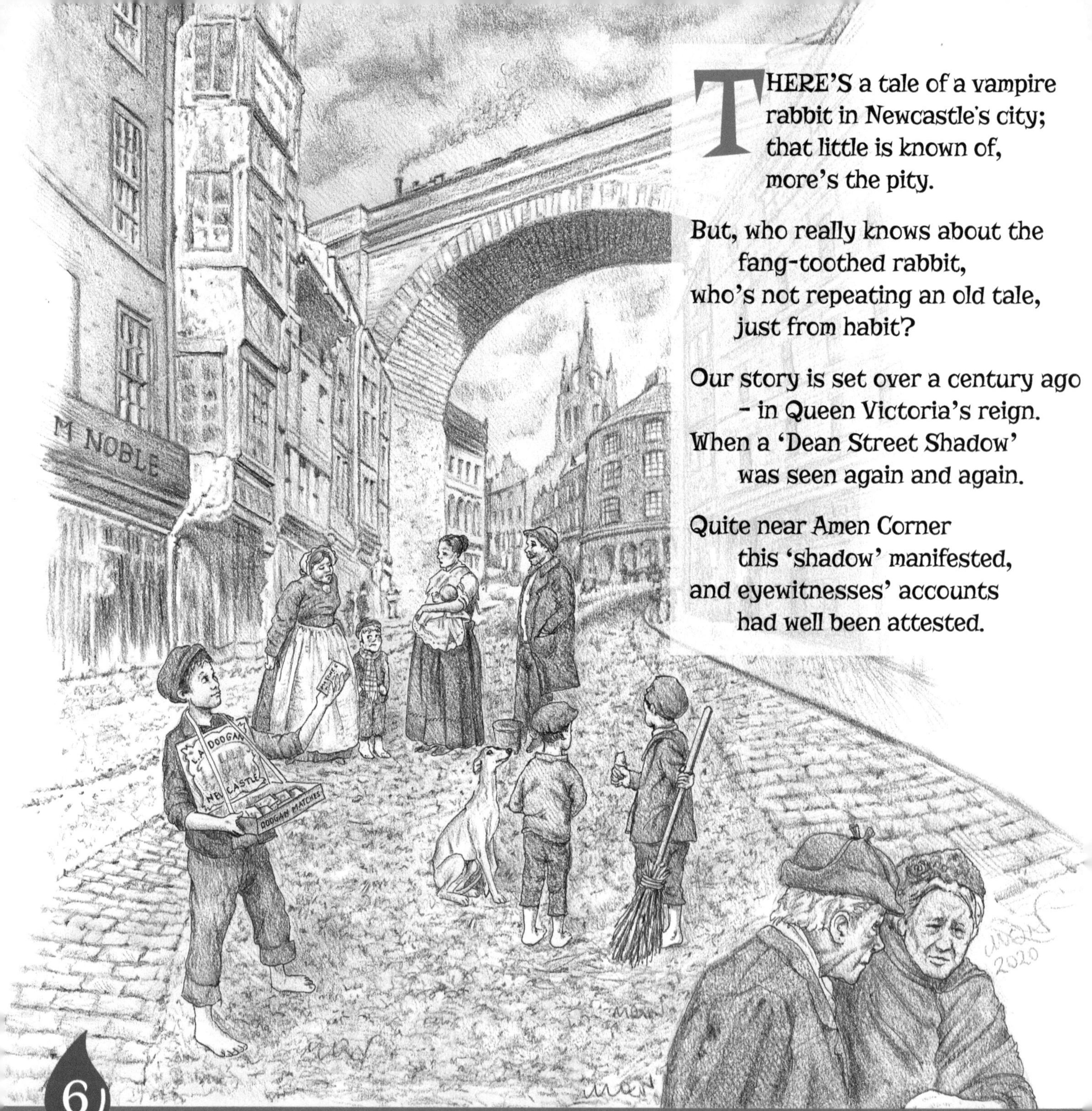
M NOBLE
NEWCASTLE
DOOGAN MATCHES

THERE'S a tale of a vampire
rabbit in Newcastle's city;
that little is known of,
more's the pity.

But, who really knows about the
fang-toothed rabbit,
who's not repeating an old tale,
just from habit?

Our story is set over a century ago
- in Queen Victoria's reign.
When a 'Dean Street Shadow'
was seen again and again.

Quite near Amen Corner
this 'shadow' manifested,
and eyewitnesses' accounts
had well been attested.

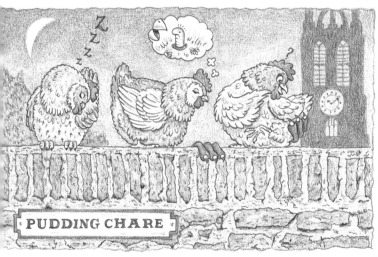

PUDDING CHARE

PUDDING CHARE

PUDDING HARE

IT was at this time many animals
went 'missing',
with cries of alarm, screams,
and much hissing!

As dusk fell...cats, dogs and chickens
were forsaken and lost,
with only the poor owners
left counting the cost.

NO creature was safe...
not even the owl or the pussy-cat,
not even a Chinese-speaking parrot,
come to that!

They all disappeared mysteriously...
...one by one,
and even the bats in the belfry
were gone.

Signs of the animals' demise
were shown by traces of gore,
creating feelings of terror
that you just couldn't ignore!

ADELAIDE
LAID
TO REST

EGLANTYNE
CALLED HOME
TO THE FINAL
HEN HOUSE

HENRIETTA
ROOST
IN PEACE

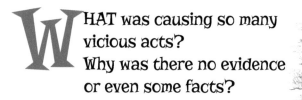

WHAT was causing so many
vicious acts?
Why was there no evidence
or even some facts?

The answer is, as we now well know,
a creature of fear -
a toothy rodent, dusty-grey
and longish-of-ear.

Soon, animals were in very
short supply,
"What else will be eaten?"
the people did cry.

POLICE NOTICE
INFORMATION REQUIRED
ON THE
'DEAN STREET SHADOW'

RESPONSIBLE FOR THE
DESTRUCTION OR MAIMING OF:
1 whippet • 5 cows
12 sheep • 11 rams
15 goats • 6 piglets • 3 ferrets
18 chickens • 8 cockerels
3 cats • 1 cockatoo • 1 parrot
4 Peruvian stick insects
If you possess any information in relation to
the 'Dean Street Shadow', please contact
Police HQ at Pilgrim Street.
There may be a reward for evidence provided.

**DISPENSARY
LANE**

CORPSES were found with the
"blood drained from the body"!
What on earth could possess
such a hideous 'hobby'?

Then, one night in the graveyard,
young Ned disappeared!
People nodded and quaked
it was as they FEARED!

The 'Shadow' had "taken"
the gravedigger's mate,
who had had muscles as large,
as a five-barred gate!

LITTLE Phoebe was next to go
'missing without trace';
the sweetest of girls
with the bonniest face...

The ghosts in the town
were quite soon 'out of sorts'.
Why? There was something
causing more terror of course!

RIP
BARRY
M. DEEP
HE WAS A GREAT
FATHER & HUSBAND
1874 - 1900

MILES
DEEP

DOUG
DEEP

ABBIE
SENIOR
1743-1832

·RIP·
DAISY
PUSHIN
1764-1855

·RIP·
COLIN
ITADAY
1776 - 1855

1820

NORAH
BONES
· R.I.P ·
1844 - 1900

10

PHANTOMS Martha Wilson and
Jack-the-Beadle at the Quayside
were highly annoyed,
it had damaged their pride!

-RIP-
Peter
Owt

1799 - 1888

-RIP-
SEAMUS
ALLOVER
1749 - 1803
and his long
suffering wife
GLADYS
ALLOVER
1752 - 1807

-RIP-
NORA
GRETZ
1801 - 1835

AMEN CORNER

QUICKLY more and more of
the toonsfolk disappeared,
but the 'Shadow' had been seen
and it was "quite long-eared"!

Shadows of "long legs" were also
glimpsed by the dim glow of a lamp;
families scurried home to safety
through the gloom and the damp.

The people of the town were scared
and how they shivered;
and even the bravest of lads
had shook and quivered.

The 'Shadow' was at last identified
as a 'sinister rabbit',
but no one volunteered to
grab it or nab it.

DOG LEAP STAIRS

WAS it really a rabbit...
or more like a hare?
The toonsfolk of the city
were too frightened to care!

Of all the nightmare creatures
this 'thing' was the worst,
a furry fiend that craved blood
to quench its thirst!

It was described as having
the most enormous jaws,
with fangs that were jagged
and red-tinged claws.

This savage rodent was also said
to sprout bat-like wings,
a creature as mythical as dragons,
griffons and 'things'.

ITS fur was unkempt...
it had scarlet eyes...
that shone like a flame,
an impossible creature to befriend or tame!

As time passed by many people
were: 'here, come and gone':
Miss Crumble, Wee Tot, Dr. Toe
and Gentleman John...

{ J. BANKS. ESQ. }

DUMFRIES
030488

THREE BATS
TEA

P&M LUPTON

CARLISLE

14

MISS Spout had been busying
herself in her quaint tea-shop,
but soon that vile bunny
caught her right 'on-the-hop'!

She hurled at its head sticky buns,
scones and stottie bread.
But, it was on that dear lady
the grim rabbit fed...

Miss Spout 'devoured' in the 'Linger Langer' tea-room!

REMAINS FOUND AMONGST STICKY
BUNS AND STOTTIES IN 'QUAINT'
PINK LANE TEA-ROOM

Miss Cordelia Spout had just
opened her quirky tea-shop in
Pink Lane in the early hours
~ yesterday, when she was
assailed by the fiendish
creature that has been
terrorising Newcastle
for the last few months...

RISING · SUN

M · SMYTH

JAPAN TEA

· TOKYO · YOKOHAMA · OSAKA · NAGOYA ·

· SAPPORO · KOBE · KYOTO · FUKUOKA ·

DURHAM
240998

WHITBY

P. WAGGOTT. Esq.

15

SQUIRE Lumley had heard
   of the ferocious bunny...
   He thought the notion
   immensely funny!

He thought himself
      so big, bold and brave:
a would-be 'hero'...
      He was digging his grave!

He went a-hunting a "cony"
      with his very big gun,
but it was a different case
      of 'run rabbit, run'!

AT twilight the city of Newcastle
became so deathly quiet,
this creature had caused
an unearthly riot!

But, the saints of the city,
in their wisdom, looked down -
with a look of concern,
which was almost a frown.

They weren't going to have good folk
bitten, bled and die,
by a wicked creature -
bloodthirsty and sly!

That fiendish rabbit
would just have to atone;
the saints stopped his antics
- they turned him to

STONE!

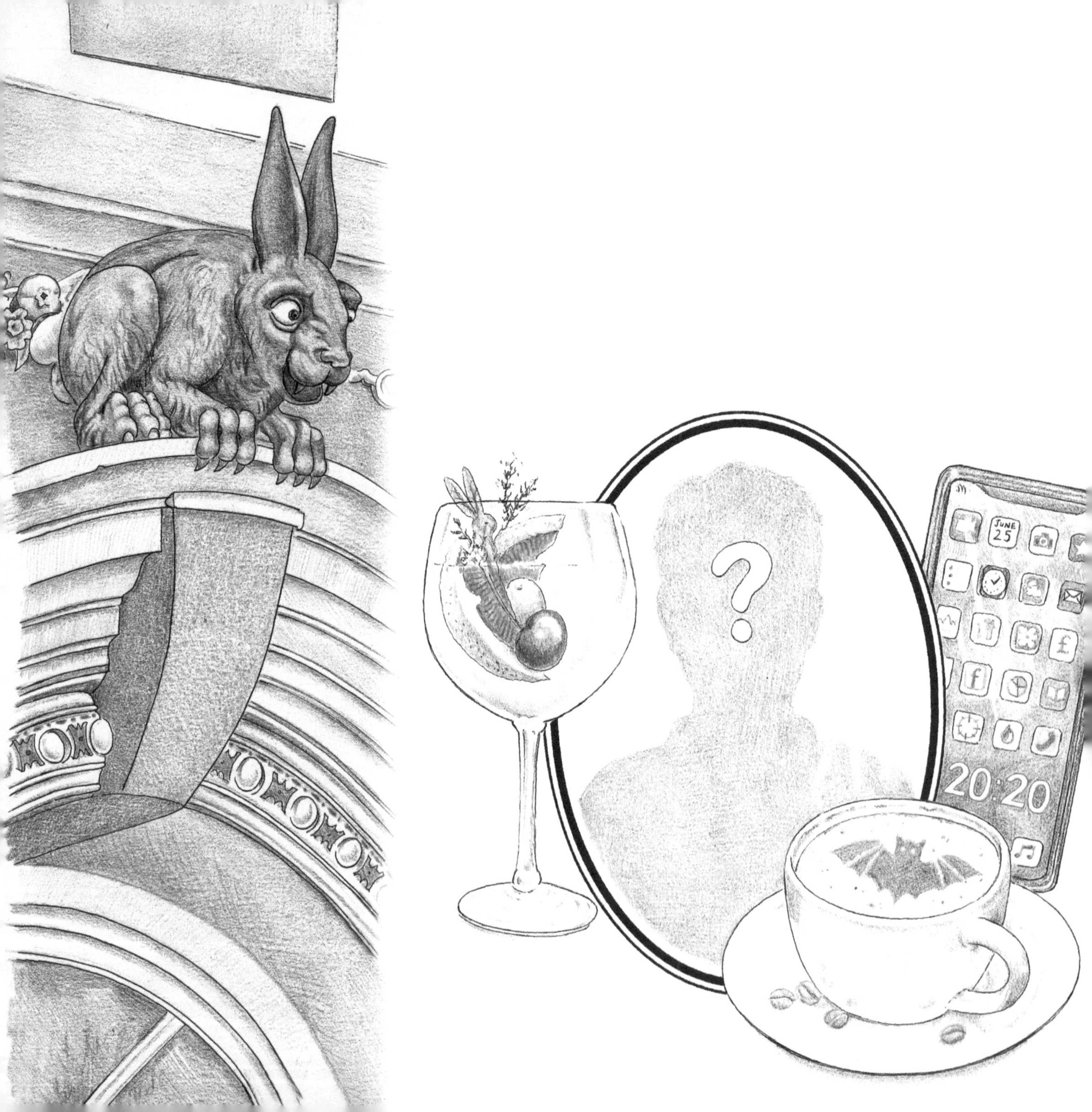
JUNE
25
20:20

Newcastle upon Tyne

2020

So, now the rabbit looks down
from a beautiful 'shelf',
where people pass by;
you may have seen him yourself.

Supposedly 'guarding' the Cathedral
graves and burial grounds,
the rabbit still sits
and no longer abounds.

For over one hundred years
he's gazed below,
seeing April's cherry blossom...
winter's falling snow...

Quashed forever his
horrible schemes...
...frozen for eternity,
or so it seems...

BUT, the day might yet come
when his imprisonment's broken
and the grotesque rodent...
is once more AWOKEN!

His stone eyes will flame and blaze
- his clay turn to hair,
consequently leading to another
terrifying affair.

So, what do you ask...
is this poem's moral?
It is: DO NOT LINGER NEAR HIM
TO KISS, LAUGH OR QUARREL!

For **YOU**,
on one moonless night,
quite unaware,
might be the next **VICTIM**
to fall in his **SNARE!**

21

-The End-

(or, is it?)

A word about the illustrations:

These illustrations were created over a period of five months, so the pressure was on to layout and illustrate the tale.
A limit on colours was set and only black (and the subsequent shades of grey) and Geranium Lake red
(and the subsequent shades of pink) were used to create a 'Gothic' effect to the scenes.

The 'Vampire Rabbit' character was created with a direct reference to the grotesque situated on the Cathedral Buildings,
Dean Street, Newcastle. The illustrations were completed whilst quaffing a great many cups of Ringtons tea
(a wonderful Newcastle-based tea and coffee company) and an abundance of custard creams,
as well as listening to the wonderful Kiki Dee and Carmelo Luggeri on my CD player.

SINK
your fangs into a good
BOOK

One of the most
amazing places
I have visited is
Newcastle's
'Lit and Phil'
(The Literary and
Philosophical Society of
Newcastle upon Tyne),
which is a great
building with
amazing staff
and lots of fantastic books.

Well worth a visit!

Acknowledgements:

Thank you to all my family and friends, who have given me encouragement over the years with regard to my art
(you know who you are), to Mary Lupton and Marie L. Smyth whom I shared my ideas with and who provided support for
this book to be written. Thank you to Simon McKay who sought advice on copyright relating to the actress Fenella Fielding.
Thank you to Vicky Boddy who provided me with an in-depth knowledge of the world of 'horror movies'
(and if there was ever a friend to ask it's this lady!).

Thank you also to Vincent J. McSherry, Cherry D. Balme and Louise A. Hobson for listening to my frustrations!
Thank you to Helene M. Phillips for all her help in providing written profiles for my art and graphic literature.
Thank you to Grosvenor House Publishing Ltd. for the support they have provided to get this book published.
Thank you to Andrea S. Daglish for being my model (with a bonnet and a parasol) for some of the images.
With acknowledgements to Vicki Storey and Barry Hutchinson for information on the Vampire Rabbit…

Character stanzas that were written, but were not incorporated into the main poem.

WEE TOT

WEE Tot was a poor,
  malnourished urchin -
his mission was simple:
  for grub he was searchin'.

But, in a dark alley
  the rabbit leapt on his back;
although the lad was little
  he was more than a snack...

FANNY CRUMBLE

MISS Crumble sold roses red
  and violets so sweet,
whilst selling in Eldon Square
  the people she'd greet.

The blood of this flaxen-haired
  maiden the rabbit did crave,
now daisies and forget-me-nots
  bloom on her grave...

DR. SEPTIMUS TOE

DR. Septimus Toe
  was a notorious 'quack';
he'd sell you brain salts
  to soothe a sore back.

Rushing to Clayton Street,
  to make a house call,
into the rabbit's clutches
  this G.P. did fall!

FOUR PERUVIAN STICK INSECTS

THE hungry rabbit saw these
  thin insects from afar;
they were clustered on some
  privet in a bell-bottomed jar.

After shaking them out - the
  insects were 'there and here';
one descended down the rabbit's
  back, one clambered up his ear!

GENTLEMAN JOHN

GENTLEMAN John in the toon
    was a well-known sight,
traipsing up 'n' down Pink Lane,
    both morning and night!

When he headed home at dusk,
    through the deepening gloom,
the furtive rabbit was waiting
    to quickly seal his DOOM!

A wee note from the Writer and Illustrator:~
I had to include a stottie in Miss Cordelia Spout's
stanzas, as it is the traditional bread of the North East
and it brings back many exquisite memories of my childhood.

Cordelia Spout

Places of interest and antiquity featured in the illustrations/graphics of this book:
The Cathedral Church of St. Nicholas *(front cover, pages 1, 5, 6, 7, 11, 17, 19, 21)*   St. Mary's Cathedral *(front cover, pages 1, 5, 19)*
Victoria Tunnel *(pages 14-15)*   Tyne Bridge *(pages 1, 19)*   Grey's Monument *(pages 1, 5, 19)*   Blackfriars *(back cover)*
Newcastle Castle *(front cover, pages 1, 5, 19, 21)*   Cathedral Buildings, Dean St. (where the Vampire Rabbit awaits YOU!) *(pages 18, 20, 21)*
~ Newcastle upon Tyne is a city that contains some truly beautiful and interesting buildings and is well worth a visit ~

25

Strawberry Place Forever

Lightning Source UK Ltd.
Milton Keynes UK
UKHW051116211120
373799UK00002B/19